DUET RECITAL SUITE SERIES

Intermediate (UK Exam Grades 3–4)

SOUTHWEST LANDSCAPES

Melody Bober

Colorado River Rapids

Sedona Sun

Majestic Grand Canyon

ISBN-10: 0-7390-5113-X
ISBN-13: 978-0-7390-5113-9

Commissioned by the Phoenix Music Teacher's Association
for their 57th Annual Piano Ensemble, 2009

Colorado River Rapids
SECONDO

Melody Bober

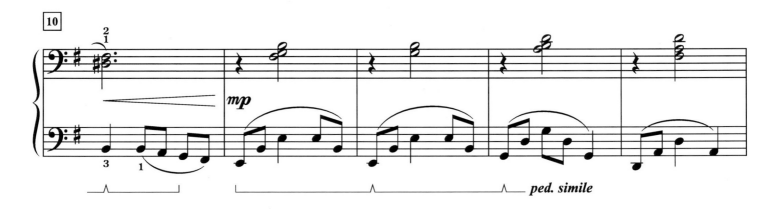

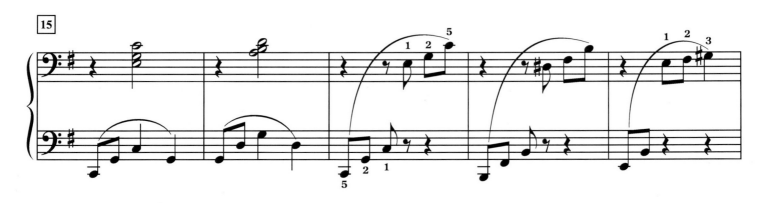

Commissioned by the Phoenix Music Teacher's Association
for their 57th Annual Piano Ensemble, 2009

Colorado River Rapids
PRIMO

Melody Bober

Swiftly (♩ = 126)
Both hands one octave higher than written throughout

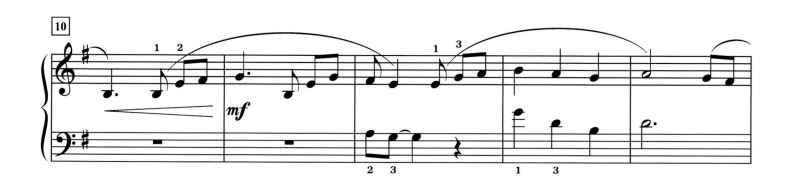

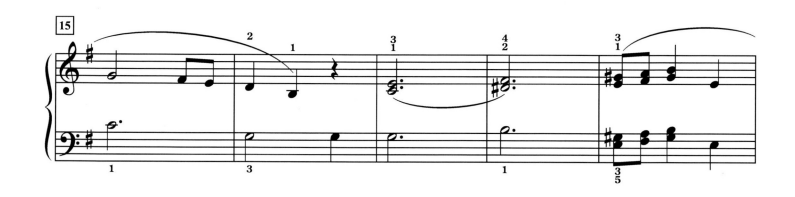

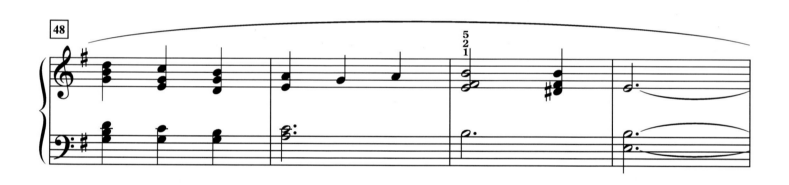

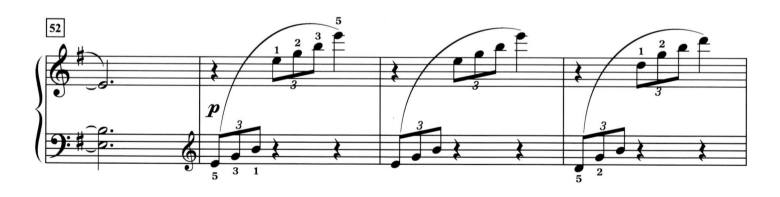

Sedona Sun
SECONDO

Melody Bober

Sedona Sun

PRIMO

Melody Bober

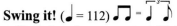

Swing it! ($\quarter$ = 112)

Both hands one octave higher than written throughout

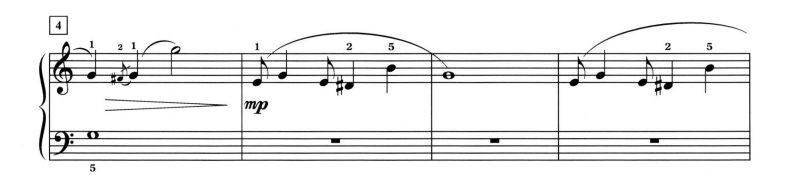

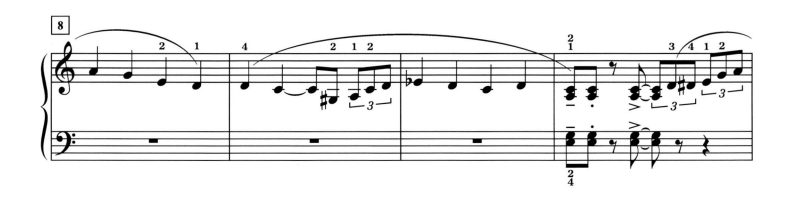

* Primo pedals in measures 31–35. Tap the rhythms on your lap, then snap or clap as directed.

* Pedal in measures 31–35, while secondo taps rhythms.

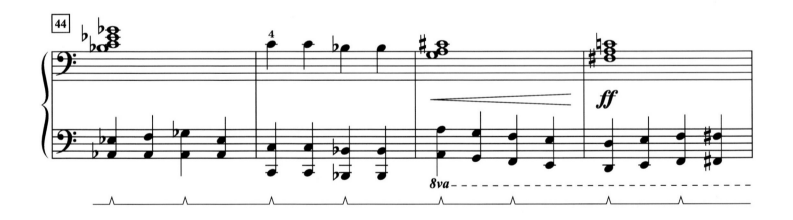

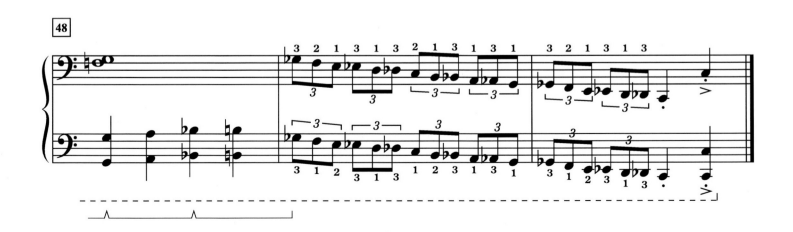

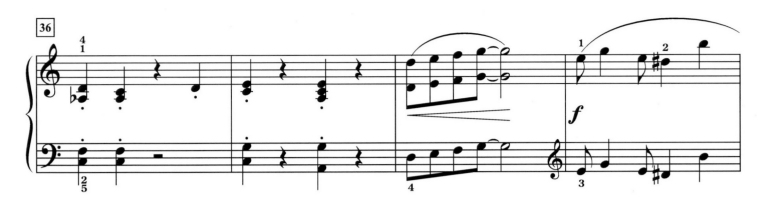

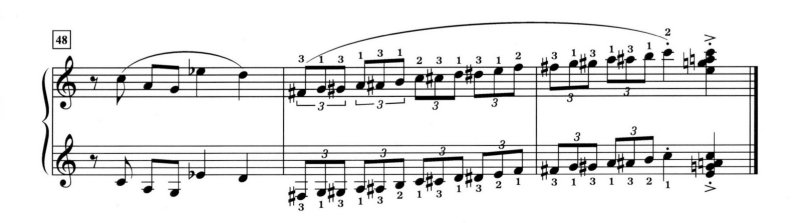

Majestic Grand Canyon
SECONDO

Melody Bober

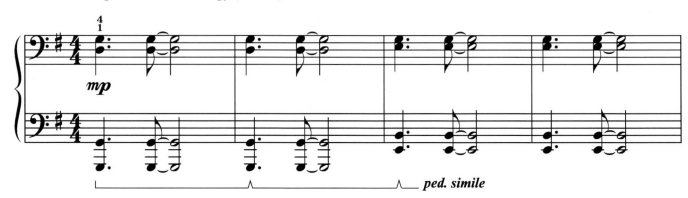

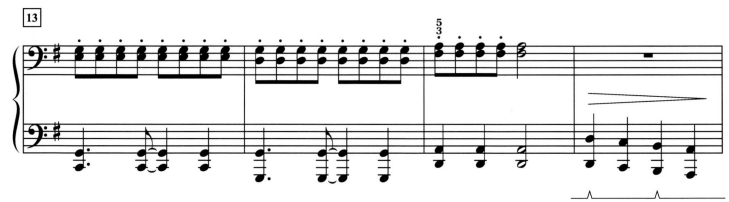

Majestic Grand Canyon

PRIMO

Melody Bober

With grandeur and energy (♩ = 132)
Both hands one octave higher than written throughout

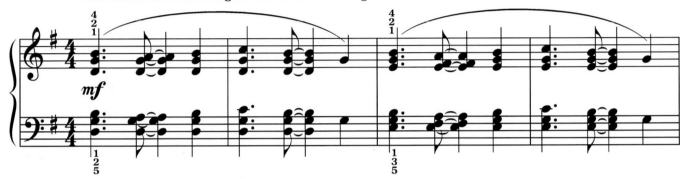

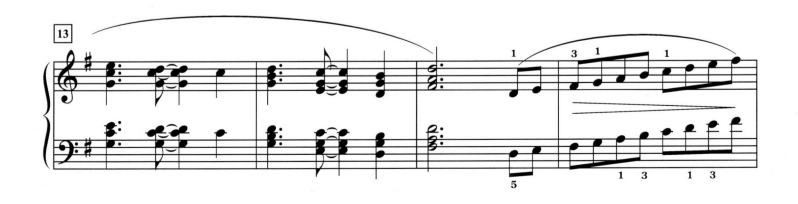

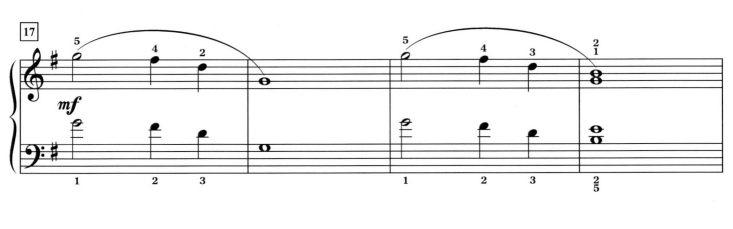

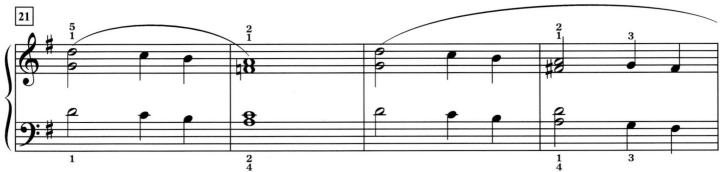

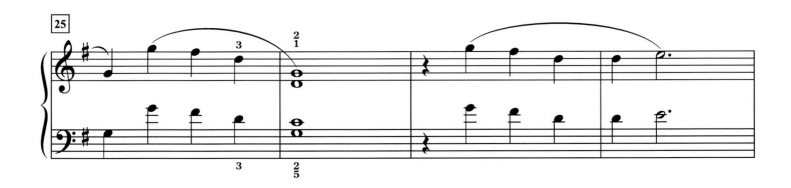

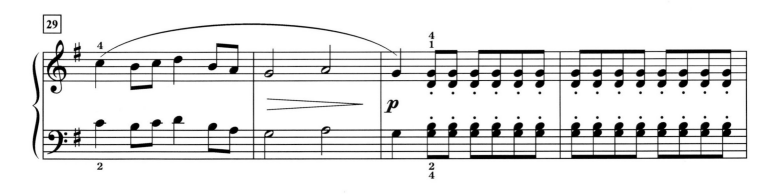

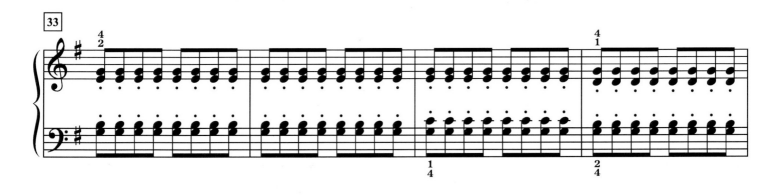

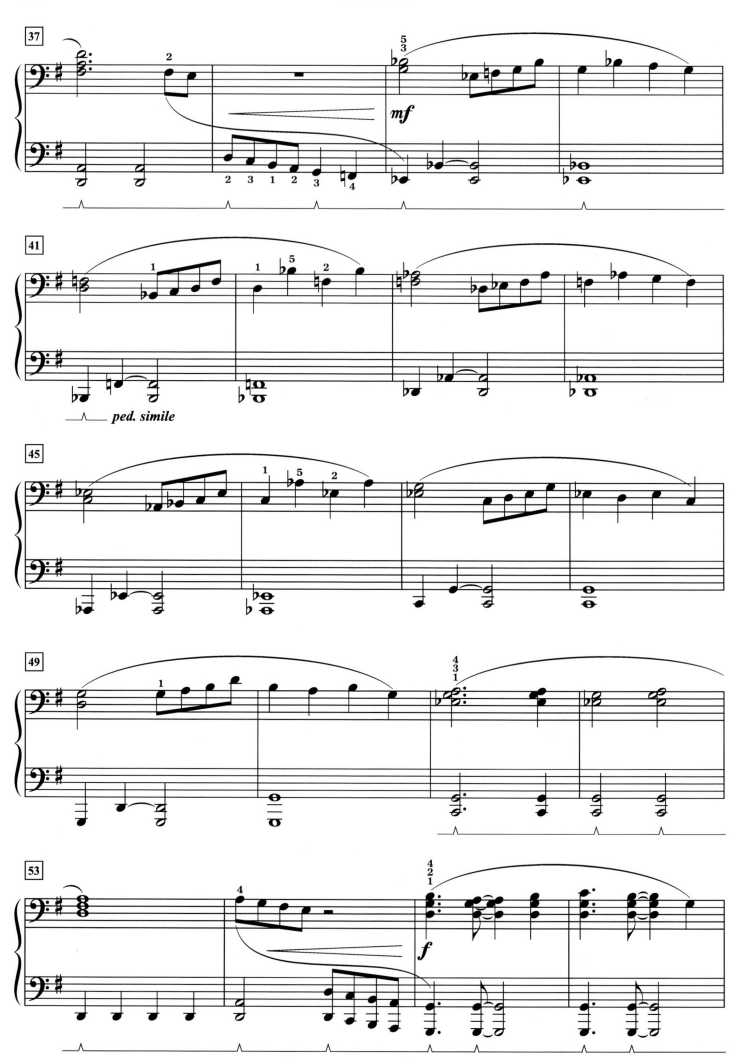

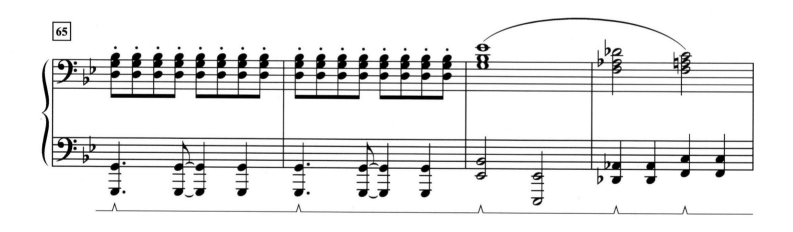

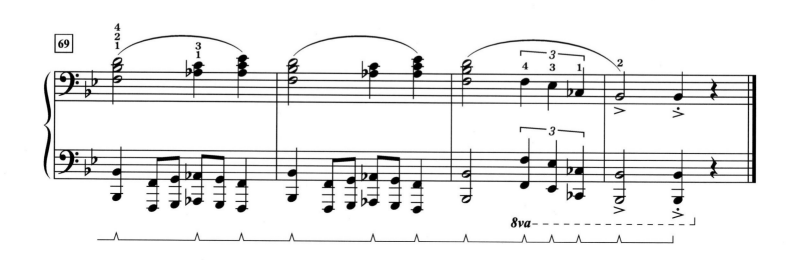